ECIA #2   Children Press 4/88   7.95
C1
2⁰⁰

D0500628

DATE DUE

Ringsley			

FOREWORD

"Frontiers of America" dramatizes some of the explorations
and discoveries of real pioneers in simple, uncluttered text.
America's spirit of adventure is seen in these early people who
faced dangers and hardship blazing trails, pioneering new
water routes, becoming Western heroes as well as legends, and
building log forts and houses as they settled in the wilderness.

Although today's explorers and adventurers face different
frontiers, the drive and spirit of these early pioneers in
America's past still serve as an inspiration.

ABOUT THE AUTHOR

During her years as a teacher and reading consultant in
elementary schools, Mrs. McCall developed a strong interest in
the people whose pioneering spirit built our nation. When she
turned to writing as a full-time occupation, this interest was the
basis for much of her work. She is the author of many books and
articles for children and adults, and co-author of elementary
school social studies textbooks.

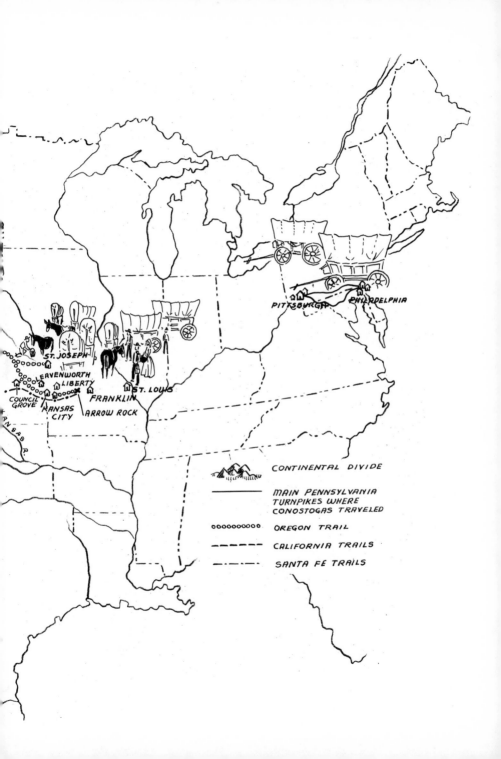

ST. JOSEPH

LEAVENWORTH
LIBERTY

COUNCIL
GROVE

KANSAS
CITY

FRANKLIN

ARROW ROCK

ST. LOUIS

KANSAS

PITTSBURGH

PHILADELPHIA

CONTINENTAL DIVIDE

MAIN PENNSYLVANIA
TURNPIKES WHERE
CONOSTOGAS TRAVELED

ooooooooooo OREGON TRAIL

CALIFORNIA TRAILS

SANTA FE TRAILS

Frontiers of America

WAGONS OVER THE
MOUNTAINS

By Edith McCall

Illustrations by Carol Rogers

℗ CHILDRENS PRESS ™

CHICAGO

Library of Congress Cataloging in
Publication Data
McCall, Edith S
    Wagons over the mountain.
    1.   The West — Hist. — Juvenile fiction.
I.   Title.
PZ7.M1229.Wag   61-10101
ISBN 0-516-03376-X

New 1980 Edition
Copyright© 1961 by Regensteiner
Publishing Enterprises, Inc.
All rights reserved. Published
simultaneously in Canada.
Printed in the United States of America.
3 4 5 6 7 8 9 10 11 12 R 87 86

CONTENTS

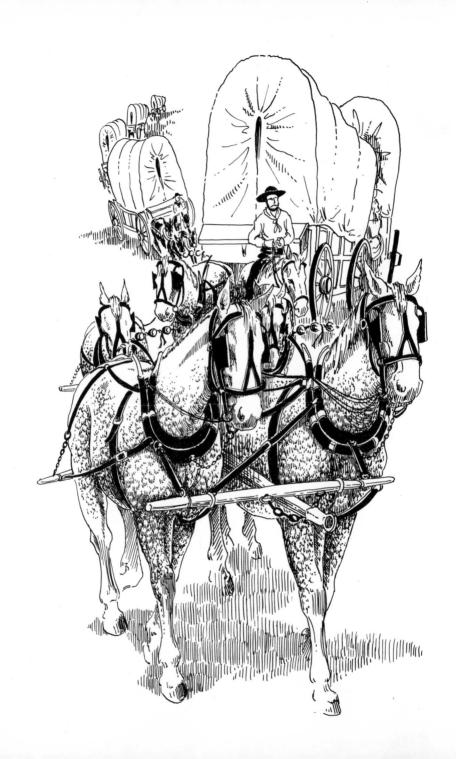

WE'LL BE THERE WITH BELLS ON

All day long, the white-topped wagons slipped and slid down the mountainside. Rumbling and creaking, dragging heavy logs behind to slow them, they bumped over rock ledges and eased around sharp curves on the narrow road. Now the sun dropped behind the next mountain ridge to the west, and the day's run was nearly over.

The road stretched ahead, clear and open to the inn in the valley where the wagoners would spend the night. The sound of the horses' hoofs was like a beating of drums in time to the music of the bells that the horses wore, hung from arches over their shoulders. Six horses pulled each of the ten big wagons. The drivers rode on the back of one horse of each "wheel" team.

The man who held the long reins of the head wagon spoke to his saddle horse.

"We'll ride up to the inn in style, Prince. Clear road ahead!" With his left hand he gave a little flick to the reins that reached to the bridles of the first pair of horses of his team. At the same moment, he raised his whip with his right hand. The whip uncurled its six feet of length, and the silk "snapper" on its end cracked above the ears of the second pair of horses, the "swing" team. His heels dug for a moment into the sides of the horse he was riding.

The gentle jangling of the bells sharpened and then was lost in the hard beat of hoofs against the stony road and the rumble of the wagon wheels. Duke, the bulldog that trotted along under the wagon all day, tied to the rear axle, yelped his excitement and set his short legs to running.

No one watching the six dapple-gray horses stepping out so briskly would have guessed that they had been pulling a load of almost four tons all day as they traveled the road from Philadelphia to Pittsburgh on the Pennsylvania frontier.

The United States was a brand new country, and Pittsburgh, the little town that was growing around Fort Pitt, seemed far, far in the west.

Each team of the ten-wagon train stepped out in its best style, following closely the wagon ahead. The innkeeper heard them coming and stepped to his doorway to see the sight.

"Get the table laid, Betsy!" he called to his wife.

"There will soon be ten hungry men to feed."

He went out into the shed in the big inn yard to empty more sacks of grain into the bins. Those sixty big horses would be hungry, too.

"Whoa!" called the driver of the lead wagon, and "Whoa!" echoed all down the line. The six dapple grays of the lead wagon slowed to a walk and turned into the inn yard. With the ease that came from doing it many times, the driver backed the wagon into the place where it would stand for the night.

Soon the inn yard was full of wagons, horses, men and dogs. Each wagoner set about the work of caring for his animals.

John, the wagoner who led the train, went to his lead team. This pair was the lightest of the three pairs. The one on the left was John's pride. She set the step the others followed, and helped him hold his place at the head of the wagon train. John gave her nose a gentle rub as he reached up to take off her arch of bells.

"You're a good old girl, Queenie," he said. The five bells he took from Queenie's back were shiny brass. The arch from which they hung was made of metal, but the wagoner had carefully wound it and

all his bell arches with black and red ribbons. Bits of the red ribbon hung from the center, matching the red plume that each of the dapple grays wore proudly atop its bridle.

The bells meant almost as much to John as his horses did. He had won them from another wagoner, fairly and squarely.

One day when the spring rains had left the road pocketed with water, his wagon train met another. This was before John had earned his place at the head of the train. He and the others in the train were forced to move over to the edge of the road. One heavily loaded wagon near the head of the train slid off into the wet clay of the ditch at the road's edge.

The wagoner worked long and hard with his team to pull the wagon back onto the road. All the other wagoners sat quietly, waiting and watching. No one offered to help, for that was the law of the road. You didn't offer to help until the wagoner in trouble gave up.

At last the wagoner unhooked the harness buckles and led his team from the wagon. Not a word was said until the team that failed walked clear of the wagon tongue. The beautiful bells gave only a few sad clangs.

"I'll pull it out!" one man called. "I need that fine set of bells!" For it was known to all that if a man had to have help, he must give his bells to the wagoner whose team could pull him out of trouble.

The wagoner unhitched his team and led it to the wagon that was stuck. He backed the team into place and hooked the harness to the wagon.

As he cracked his whip, the six horses leaned into their work. The wagon wheels made part of a turn. Then one of the horses slipped a little and the wheels rolled back. Twice more the wagoner urged his team to pull. But he had to give up. The other wagoners jeered and laughed as he led his team away.

John got down from his saddle. He walked up to Queenie. Queenie was very young then, and John was new in the business of wagoning. He had used all the money he earned to buy the matched dapple grays, one at a time as he found them. As yet, no bell arches hung over their shoulders.

"Think we can do it, Queenie?" John asked, and Queenie tossed her head as if she could do anything. John called out, "I'll give it a try!"

Soon he had his team in place. The wagon was tipping badly as its right rear wheel sank deeper into the mud. But John was quite sure his team could pull it out, for each horse knew how to work with the others.

"Forward ho-o!" he cried and cracked his whip. Each horse leaned hard. Even the wagoner's dog seemed to be trying to help as he leaned into his collar, almost choking himself.

The wagon wheels began to make that one important turn. It was as if one giant machine worked to pull that wagon from the mud. Little by little, the wheels turned. One turn, another faster one, and the wagon moved forward.

"Whoa!" cried John, and the men broke into a cheer.

John unhitched his team. Without looking, he knew that the other wagoner was taking off his set of bells. John whistled softly as he hooked the harness back onto his own wagon. In a moment the wagoner was beside him.

"They're yours, John," was all he said, but John knew how the other man felt. His team had worn those bells proudly for many years. They had been won, long ago, just as John's younger, stronger team had won them today.

His hands shaking, John set the bell-hung arches over his team for the first time. The higher toned smaller bells went over the lead team. The swing team wore the two sets of middle-sized bells which gave a deeper ring to blend with the smaller bells. There were four of these on each arch.

The wheel horse that pulled beside John's saddle horse wore the set of three large bells which had an even deeper tone. John grinned as he snapped this last arch into place. He jumped into the saddle and picked up the reins as the other wagoners gave another cheer.

Then the lead wagoner started forward. John heard the pleasant ringing of his own bells for the first time. His team sensed his pride and stepped out smartly. From that day on, John could call out with the other proud owners of bell teams as they started on a journey, "We'll be there with bells on!"

He had never lost his set of bells, for his team never failed him, no matter how rough the going.

The end-of-the-day work was always the same, yet always new. When the six horses were watered, John took the feed trough from its place at the rear of the wagon, filled it with grain, and placed it on the wagon tongue. He led his horses, now wearing only halters, to the trough and tied three to each side of the wagon tongue.

As the horses ate, John took a pine tar bucket from its hook near the back of the wagon. The cover had a hole in the middle, through which the handle of a paddle was stuck. A paddleful of the sticky stuff went into the hub of each red wheel to grease it. A little more went on the rubbing plate, up where the front axle turned. He checked the three-inch-wide iron tires on the wheels and found a loose nail to drive into place again.

At last the wagon stood ready for the next day's travel. The canvas cover was stretched tight over the six wooden arches that held it in place. The ropes reached down over red sideboards set above the blue wagon body.

The wagonbox was curved, rising a little at each end. This was to keep the load of goods from sliding too easily to one end or the other when the wagon was on a steep hill. The wagons were made for the mountain-road trade. They were called Conestoga wagons, named for the creek which ran through Lancaster County in southeastern Pennsylvania where they were made.

The night's work was nearly finished. John had one more job to do. He took his ax from the fish-shaped iron hanger on the side of the wagon. He would need a good sharp ax the next day to cut young trees for braking poles. These would go into the wheels when they started down the last mountainside on the road to Pittsburgh. There was a grindstone in the yard and John soon made the sparks fly as he held the ax to the turning wheel.

Then he was ready to join the other wagoners around the plank table in the big room of the inn. A big meal, rough talk and tall story telling for a while and then it would be time for each man to go out to his wagon to take the meat scraps and bones to the dogs and to bring in his bedroll. The dogs would keep watch over the horses all night while the men slept on the inn floor near the big fireplace. Dawn would come soon enough, and the men would be back in the saddle again, ready to urge their teams over the mountains ahead.

At Pittsburgh, flatboats waited to take some of the

wagonloads of goods down the Ohio River to the pioneers who were building their settlements in the land beyond the mountains. The wagon trains were playing their part in helping the new United States of America to grow strong.

"We'll be there with bells on!" the wagoners called time and time again, and set out to take their white-topped wagons westward over the mountains.

Westward over the mountains those Conestoga wagons would go until at last they reached the end of the mountains at the Pacific Ocean's shore. But that would take a long, long time. The new United States of America would be as old as an old, old man before Pacific shores were reached.

FROM BOONE'S LICK ROAD
TO SANTA FE

Westward moved the frontier. Over the eastern mountains and down the Ohio Valley it went, and up and down the Mississippi. It started up the Missouri River, but it did not go far.

Past the place where Kansas City is today, the plains began and there the government had put the Indians. No pioneer could settle there, nor in all the land from Texas to California. The whole Southwest belonged to Mexico.

Where the frontier went, wagons were not far behind. Boats went first, nosing up the rivers and into the side streams. Pack horses followed Indian and buffalo trails. But as soon as settlers' cabins dotted the land, the trails were widened for wagons.

When the United States was about forty-five years old, the town farthest west was Franklin, Missouri. Daniel Boone's sons had gone up the Missouri River for about a hundred miles from the fur traders' towns of St. Louis and St. Charles. They found the trails of buffalo and deer which led to a "salt lick" not far from where Franklin was to grow. There, salt water bubbled from the earth as a spring and left the salt the wild animals found and licked from the rocks.

"We can get enough salt here to supply all the people around St. Charles, and maybe some to sell in St. Louis, too," Nathan and Daniel Morgan Boone decided. So they widened a trail all the way from St. Charles to the salt springs. "Boone's Lick Road" it was called, and soon pioneers were following it in their farm wagons covered like Conestoga freighters of Pennsylvania. One of the first wagons carried a family named Carson. Little Kit Carson, just a baby when he rode west to Franklin in a wagon, grew up to be one of the most famous men of the West.

Kit was ten or eleven when Franklin became the beginning of the Santa Fe Trail. It was on this famous trail that the first wagon train traveled across the great West.

One of the people who came to Franklin to live was Captain William Becknell. He had been an officer in the War of 1812, and had lived an exciting life. After the war, he needed a new way to make a living.

One day, Captain Becknell rode west of Franklin to the cabin of old Zeke Williams. William Becknell liked to talk with Zeke, for Zeke had been all over the West in the years that he had been a fur trapper. Zeke's talk of how the Comanches in the Southwest captured wild horses and mules to sell to white traders gave the captain an idea.

"Zeke, how much did you say a man could get mules for out in Comanche country?" he asked.

"Two, maybe three dollars' worth of stuff to trade," Zeke said. "Bring those mules back here and they'll bring seventy-five dollars a head."

"That's what I aim to do, Zeke," said the captain. "Show me again the best way to go."

Zeke scratched out a map in the dust before the doorstep of his cabin.

"But remember," he told Becknell, "the Spanish don't want to let you trade there. The last American trader that went into Mexican country landed in jail. Stay clear of Santa Fe. That's where the government officers are, and they're sure to catch you."

In September of that year, 1821, Captain Becknell, his brother, Tom, and a little group of men left Franklin. They led seventeen pack horses, loaded with goods that had come up from St. Louis on the steamboat. Bright colored cloth, beads, knives, and the usual things that Indians wanted from the white man were in the packs.

There was a man who took people and their horses across the Missouri River on his flatboat about twelve miles west of Franklin at a place called Arrow Rock. From there, the pack train headed west toward the place where Kansas City is now, followed the Kansas River a few miles, and then swung southwest to the Arkansas River valley. This was the path that became the Santa Fe Trail.

Becknell and his train followed the Arkansas until the Rocky Mountains came into sight in Colorado. Then they headed south, hoping to reach Comanche country without having to go into the mountains. They followed a river valley, as Zeke told them to, but the farther they went the rougher the country became. They found themselves in the mountains, following narrow paths through the valleys.

Sometimes great rocks barred the way. They spent hours clearing a way for the pack horses.

It grew very cold, and snow fell in the mountains. Both men and horses ran out of food.

On the morning of November 13, Captain Becknell had to tell the men that he was lost.

"We'll starve if we just sit here," the men said. "If we head south, maybe we'll find our way to Santa Fe."

"And end in jail," Captain Becknell said. "But at least we won't starve in jail, and it can't be this cold."

Later that same day, the men heard voices and the sound of horses' hoofs coming toward them.

"The Spanish soldiers!" Captain Becknell said. He didn't know whether to be glad there was someone to show them the way out of the mountains or sad because they would have to go to jail. He walked forward to meet the men.

But the leader did not point his gun at the traders. Instead, he smiled and held out his hand. For these were not Spaniards, but Mexican soldiers who had been fighting to win Mexico's freedom from Spain. Becknell talked with the Mexicans, mostly in signs. When he turned to his waiting men, they knew the news was good.

"They'll take us to Santa Fe, but not to go to jail!" he said. "The Mexicans want the American traders to come to their city, now that the Spanish rulers are gone."

The Comanches and their mules were forgotten. The men followed the soldiers to Santa Fe.

The traders were surprised at how many silver dollars the black-haired, dark-eyed people of the old Mexican city were willing to pay for their goods. Cloth for which the men paid twenty cents a yard was sold for three silver dollars. They quickly sold all the goods they had and bought mules with part of the money. They headed back home with the animals and plenty of cash, too. The Santa Fe trade was opened.

Becknell and his brother were talking over plans for another trip as soon as springtime came.

"We can take more goods if we use wagons," the captain said.

"Now, Bill," said Tom Becknell, "you haven't forgotten the mountain passes. How could we take wagons through them?"

"We don't have to go that way," Becknell answered. "The Mexicans said that the mountains end not many miles south of Santa Fe. We may have to travel more miles, but we can swing around the high mountains and take wagons all the way."

As Zeke had done, Bill Becknell scratched out a map in the dust. "Instead of following the Arkansas River all the way west, we cut southwest about here." He jabbed at his dusty map. "The Mexicans say there is another river farther south that we can follow—the Cimarron."

Captain Becknell did not know that he would be trading the troubles of the mountain pass for another kind of trouble. He ordered three big freight wagons from Pittsburgh.

The three big Conestogas were loaded onto the boats leaving Pittsburgh early in that spring of 1822. Down the Ohio they came, then up the Mississippi to St. Louis. Captain Becknell went there to meet them and to buy goods to load them. He bought many yards of the cloth the Mexicans liked, and pots and pans, knives and rifles, and other things he thought he could sell at a good price. Then the wagons were pulled to St. Charles and over Boone's Lick Road to Franklin.

It was May 22 when the first little wagon train headed west to cross the Great Plains. There were twenty-one men riding horseback, the three wagons, each drawn by six mules, and more mules with packs on their backs. Instead of three hundred dollars' worth of goods, Captain Becknell brought three thousand dollars' worth this trip. Even though another pack train left Franklin earlier in the spring, Captain Becknell was sure he could sell it all.

It took the little flatboat at Arrow Rock twelve trips to carry all the men, horses, mules and wagons across the Missouri River. Then on to the west the train went, following the same trail Becknell followed before.

The Indians who saw the wagons stared at the great, white-topped moving "houses." They had never seen a wagon. They had not learned to use wheels to help them. When they had something to move, they loaded it onto a travois, which was simply two poles dragged along by a horse.

The creeks gave the men some trouble. On the plains, the creeks cut deep trenches with straight sides. The men had to break down the banks enough for the wagons to ease their way down and then up again. But the going was quite easy until after they left the Arkansas River valley to find the Cimarron River.

There was no trail to follow over the plains and sand hills. No one had told them that this stretch of land was dry as a bone. The men ran out of water in two days' time.

The summer sun seemed to dare the men to go on. Sweat ran from men and mules alike. Gray dust settled on them. From morning until night, there was no shade in which man or mule could rest.

"The Cimarron should be in that valley just ahead," Captain Becknell said. "And the river will be a welcome sight!"

With high hopes, the men went toward the valley. The big wheels of the Conestogas made ribbons over the low ridges along the way. At last there were no more ridges, and they were in the wide valley.

But only the dry bed of what may have been a stream in wet weather was at the valley's bottom.

"I must have been wrong," Captain Becknell said. "The Cimarron must be in the next valley."

Hope helped them last through another night without water. Hope helped them climb more ridges the next morning until they could see where the next valley lay.

"Look!" cried one of the men. "A lake!"

He pointed to a stretch of shimmering water not too far ahead. The men's tongues were growing thick, and the mules and horses were hardly able to travel, but the sight of the lake helped them move on.

And then it was gone. Nothing but more dusty, dry earth with a few wilted weeds growing in it lay ahead.

Captain Becknell shook his head. "It was a mirage.

Just a mirage, a trick that layers of hot air play on your eyes."

The men sat in their saddles in silence. Hopelessly, they stared at the place where that lovely "lake" had been. Then Captain Becknell spoke. His voice was as cracked and dry as the riverbed.

"The Cimarron has to be just ahead. Come on, men. It must be over the next ridge."

They eased the wagons over the ridge and down into another valley. A riverbed lay at the bottom. It was plain to see that the hot, bare rocks and the sand had been washed by water in the past. But there was no water now.

The men, too discouraged and sick to do more, lay down on the bare earth. One or two took dry biscuits from their packs and tried to eat. But they could not swallow. The salty, dried meat they had was of little use. It would only make them thirstier.

"We'll have to turn back to the Arkansas," Captain Becknell decided. "We'll start when you are ready, men."

But no one had the strength to put the packs onto the mules.

"Sure looks like a buffalo over there," one of the

men said, pointing up the river valley. "I'm seeing things again."

"I see it, too," said another man. "He's a pretty sad looking fellow, but he looks real to me."

Even a lean old buffalo would have juices in his body that could mean life to thirsty men.

"I think he's real," Becknell said. "Let's creep up close enough to shoot him."

He and three other men crawled toward the animal. If they frightened him into running, they would never be able to get him.

When they were sure their rifle shots could reach the buffalo, Becknell said, "Ready! Take aim,—fire!"

The buffalo's knees buckled. He fell forward.

One of the men had been on the plains enough to know what to look for. If the buffalo had come from a water hole, there would be water in his stomach. They took a knife and set to work to find out.

"He must have just come from drinking," they decided. "Canteens. Give us your canteens!" they called to the other men.

Three of the strongest men set out with the canteens. They had no trouble following the buffalo's trail. Into the dry river valley they went, and on up the streambed. There, a mile or so upriver, they found a pool of water.

Never had water tasted so good! It was warm from the sun, but that mattered not at all. When they had satisfied their thirst, one man began filling canteens while a second man opened and closed the tops. The third man began to poke into the sand near the pool with his rifle. As the rifle made a hole, water began to fill the hole.

"Look," he called to the others. "There's water under this riverbed instead of in it."

They dug a larger hole, going down until they reached wet sand. The water came into the hole as before.

The first wagon train to the west had been very near to ending its journey there in the desert. But soon it was moving on. The men found that they could usually find enough water, either in pools in the riverbed or by digging under it.

Mountains rose ahead of them that seemed to go on and on to the south. Becknell, afraid their food would be gone if they looked too long for the way around the mountains, decided to cross them at the best pass he could find. But the place he chose was so steep that

they had to take the wagons apart and haul the goods up with ropes.

Wheels, wagon beds and all went up the mountain, too. When the trail widened, the men put them back together again. The first wagon train went on.

One day they saw the valley where the old Mexican city lay. Down toward the buildings of sun-baked bricks they went. The three Conestogas groaned and creaked all the way. Rumbling and rattling, the first American wagons ever seen in Santa Fe entered the square "plaza" in the town's center.

"Los Americanos!" the cry rose, and the sleepy city came to life. Soon it was like a carnival, for the Mexicans had never before seen so much treasure as that which came from the big, white-topped Conestogas.

The Santa Fe Trail saw many a wagon train in the years to come. By 1824, a way to take the wagons around the mountains instead of over them was marked on the maps. Big water barrels were put on the wagons to help men and animals over the dry stretches.

Wagon trains, in the years ahead, would play a big part in the opening of the West.

INDIANS WHO WOULD NOT GO AWAY

There were more than one hundred wagons, mostly big Conestoga freighters, in the wagon train that headed west on the Santa Fe Trail in 1831. It was only ten years since Captain Becknell had opened the trail, but so many wagons were being used in the west that a St. Louis company had begun to make Conestogas.

Even the fur traders who used the northern trail were taking wagons as far as the mountains.

The frontier had moved, too. The wild, muddy Missouri River went over its banks in 1828 and washed busy Franklin right off the map. The starting point for the Santa Fe Trail moved west then to the new town of Independence, Missouri, at the big bend of the Missouri River.

For two weeks in the middle of May, 1831, wagons had been moving out of Independence. A few left at a time, heading for Council Grove. This was a stretch of woods about a half-mile wide along a Kansas creek, about one-hundred-fifty miles west of Independence. By May 26, all the wagons of the big train were there.

That night, the wagoners chose a captain. His name was Stanley, and he would lead the train on the long journey over the plains. He divided the train into four divisions. The men of each division elected a lieutenant to lead them.

It was early afternoon on May 27 when the wagon train was ready to head out into the plains where no white man lived.

"Catch up!" called Captain Stanley.

"Catch up! Catch up!" called each lieutenant.

"Hooray! Hooray!" shouted the men, and hurried to harness their teams. This was the call that meant they would move out of camp as soon as they could get ready. The woods were noisy with the excited voices of the men who were making the journey for the first time and the stern orders of those who knew how a wagon train should be run.

Mules balked, braying out their feelings about leaving their fine pasture for the hard work of the trail. Wagons creaked and rumbled as they were moved into their places in the four lines.

"All's set!" called out the leader of the first section that was lined up and ready.

"All's set!" called another lieutenant a moment

later. The third call soon followed.

As soon as the fourth "All's set!" was heard, the captain spurred his horse to gallop to the head of the line.

"STRE-ETCH OUT!" he called back.

Whips cracked. Drivers cried, "Hep, hep!" "Get along, there!" "Gee-yup!" "Giddy-ap!" or whatever their animals answered to. The train was on its way.

It stretched out in a double line. Later, when the trail was very wide, there would be four lines. But all the way to Santa Fe, through the Indian country, the wagons would stay together.

There were no jingling, merry bells on the teams that pulled these wagons. Bells would tell too much in enemy Indian country. And these teams weren't the high-stepping, beautifully matched horses of the Pennsylvania roads. They were mostly hard-working mules and slow, plodding oxen, six or eight to a wagon.

There were horses, too, but most of them belonged to the sportsmen who came along just for the adventure and rode in light wagons called "dearborns." The dearborn had a regular top instead of the canvas-covered wooden hoops. It had side curtains that rolled down to keep out some of the rain. Horses also pulled two small cannons on wheels.

On they went, the wagoners in flannel shirts of bright colors with leather vests over them, and rough cloth trousers tucked into heavy boots. Some had coats of the homespun cloth called "blue jean." The sportsmen had "city" clothes, topped with fancy hunting jackets. A few frontiersmen went west with the train, too, in their buckskins. There were even a few Mexicans in bright Spanish dress, taking their black-haired ladies home to Santa Fe after a visit in the United States.

Rattlesnakes, high water in the rivers, and buffalo herds gave the train some trouble, but things went fairly well until they reached the place where they were to leave the Arkansas River valley and head for the Cimarron. They had seen some Indians, but they were from friendly tribes.

The wagons stopped and formed the big square they always made at night. Each side of the square was made up of one division. The middle space was a corral where the animals were kept until it was time to stake them out to feed on the prairie grass.

"Fill up the water kegs!" the lieutenants ordered.

Outside the square, the cooks built their fires, using

the dry grass and buffalo "chips," all they had for fuel this far west. Usually, the other men rested while the cooks broiled the buffalo steaks, but this night they went to the river again and again, bringing up all the water they could carry with them.

"There may be water ahead of us," Captain Stanley told the men who had never gone this way before, "and again there may not. We may have to travel forty miles or more without seeing a drop. You never know about the Cimarron."

And so, when the men rolled up in their blankets on the ground near the dying campfires that night, they felt ready for the desert miles ahead. But it was hard to go to sleep, for they knew that in the morning a new and different part of the journey would begin. The easy miles were behind them, and the hard ones ahead. Ahead, too, lay the country where warring Indian tribes might be meeting in battle. Real trouble could be waiting for the train.

They journeyed on, and they found the trouble. But it was not from desert dryness, for a sudden, unusual summer rain put water into the streams. After the storm, the sun seemed hotter than ever, as if it were trying to take back that gift of water as fast as it could.

It seemed as if time for the noon stop would never come.

"There may be water in the riverbed," Captain Stanley said. "We'll stop where the animals can drink."

The team of oxen pulling one of the big freighters smelled the water ahead and broke into a run as they went over the last sandhill before the stream.

"Whoa!" cried the wagoner. He ran to the lead team, but he could not catch up. The wagon toppled crazily as the animals hurried into the water. As they stopped to drink, the big Conestoga tipped, and over it went. It lay on its side, the water quickly graying the white top.

"My goods!" cried the wagoner. "All my goods will be ruined!"

Everyone rushed in to help. With ropes and mules, the wagon was set upright again. Then, while the cooks got the noon meal ready, all hands set to work unrolling yards and yards of bright colored cloth all over the sandhills.

The wagon trouble did not come alone. While

everyone was busy rescuing the goods, the cry came, "Indians!"

A party of horsemen was in plain sight at the top of the next ridge, coming toward the wagon camp.

"Take your places inside the corral!" ordered Captain Stanley. "Rifles ready, but don't fire until I give the signal!"

But as the Indians came over the last rise, some of the men put their rifles to their shoulders. "Hold your fire!" cried Captain Stanley, as he jumped to his feet.

The men saw the reason. Leading the Indians was one who carried a pole. From it waved a flag.

"It's the Stars and Stripes! This is not a war party!" Captain Stanley said. He put down his rifle and went out to meet the Indians. The four lieutenants followed him.

There were about eighty Sioux Indians on the rise just above the wagon camp sitting quietly on their horses. Captain Stanley and the Indian chief talked together in sign language. Anxiously, the wagoners waited for the "talk" to be finished.

At last, Captain Stanley and the lieutenants stepped back. The Indians wheeled about on their ponies, and

in a moment only a cloud of dust showed where they had been.

"They came to warn us," Captain Stanley said when he was back in the wagon camp. "As I understand it, there are thousands of Indians on the trail ahead of us. Blackfeet or Comanches. Either one, this chief seemed to feel that they would be on the warpath against us."

No one slept soundly that night, even though Captain Stanley posted double guard. But morning came without any sign of more Indians.

The next day, the train was moving slowly along the Cimarron when the scouts, who had ridden ahead, hurried back to report to Captain Stanley.

"A band of warriors heading this way!" they called.

"Form the corral!" ordered Captain Stanley.

As quickly as they could, the wagoners formed their square, turning wagon tongues inward so that the teams were inside. The two cannons were wheeled into the best position. The men checked their rifles and dropped down to fire from between and under the wagons.

They were nervous. "My gun's empty!" one man cried, and hurried back to his wagon for powder and bullets.

"The powder got wet!" came another cry.

"I rammed down a ball without powder!" cried another.

"Can't find my flint!"

It seemed that about half of the men could not get their muzzle loading rifles ready for action.

Captain Stanley was watching through his spyglass for the first Indians to appear. He saw them, topping a ridge, riding their ponies hard. Some of the men saw them, too, and held their rifles ready to fire.

"Hold your fire!" Captain Stanley ordered sternly. "I mean it. *Don't fire unless I signal!* They may be on a peaceful errand."

"They don't look it," said one of the men. He was one who was on his first journey west.

Captain Stanley said, "Don't let the way they look fool you. They almost always ride up as if they meant to kill every last man of us. If you fire at them, they will, too."

The men kept their rifles ready, but none fired as the band of painted warriors drew near. The Indians had bows and arrows ready. With shrieks and whoops, they circled around the wagon train. The men spread out, watching from each side of the square, waiting for the moment when the first arrow would fly toward the wagons. When that moment came, Captain Stanley told them, and not a moment sooner, they could fire.

But no arrow flew. After three trips around the wagon camp, the Indians lined up their ponies facing the wagons and sat quietly. An Indian who wore a long, bright red coat seemed to be the chief.

The silence of the next minute froze each living being, even the animals crowded inside the square. Then a donkey brayed. At the same moment the red-coated chief spoke to the brave on the pony beside his. The brave handed his chief a long-stemmed, feather trimmed peace pipe. The grip of fear was broken, and a deep sigh went through the camp.

Captain Stanley knew the plains and the people who lived on them as well as he knew how to move a wagon train across the land.

"Parade formation," he said, and each old-time wagoner knew what to do. One hurried to his wagon and pulled out a small drum and a pair of drumsticks. Another reached into his pack for a fife. A third unrolled an American flag from its pole. While the Indians watched, the wagoners opened one side of their corral and, guns on shoulders, marched out to the beat of the drum.

The fife player began to play *Yankee Doodle* in high, shrill tones. The first-time journeyers caught the idea and fell into step at the end of the parade.

Flag waving, drum beating, and fife whistling, the men marched in double line around the wagon train. Captain Stanley, remembering his days as a soldier in the War of 1812, led the parade to a position in full view of the Indians.

"Company, halt! One, two!" he cried. Then, "Right face, one two!" and his men stood in a double row, facing the line of braves on their ponies. The captain walked forward to meet the chief. Without a smile, he took the pipe the chief offered him and drew deeply on it.

He passed the pipe back to the chief and made signs for the braves to move back and that his men would do the same. The chief nodded in understanding. The braves backed off and the wagoners marched inside their corral. White and Indian leaders faced each other alone.

As the men moved inside the corral, one of them caught sight of another group of Indians coming. This band was far larger than the first. Nervously they watched.

Captain Stanley and the red-coated chief were still talking in hand signs when the oncoming body of Indians topped the next rise.

"Must be a thousand of them," one of the men said. "How can we hold off that many if they attack us?"

"Luck is with us," one old wagoner said. "Look closely, and you will see that many of them are women and children. This is a tribe moving from one place to another. Warriors don't like to attack when their families are near. If we are careful not to anger them, we may get through this safely."

At last Captain Stanley came back. "If any man fires his rifle, whether he hits an Indian or not, it may mean death to all of us," he warned the company. "We'll make noon camp here, but keep careful watch at all times. I am not yet sure what it is they want of us, but the chief claims they come in peace."

The Indians, too, were making camp. The men could see that the women were setting up the tepees, which they carried on their travois—poles tied to the horses' sides and dragged along the ground with a buffalo hide stretched between them to hold goods.

The poles were set up first, and then the coverings, made of skins sewed together, were unfolded and pulled around the poles. There were about five hundred tepees standing when the work was finished.

An hour or two later, Captain Stanley decided to move the train on. Perhaps they could leave the Indians behind and see no more of them.

"Catch up!" he called.

The teams had not been unharnessed, so it took only a few minutes for the "All set!" calls to come. The wagon train stood in formation, four lines of twenty-eight or twenty-nine wagons each. One cannon was put at the head of the train this time, and one behind it. The extra horses, mules and oxen at the end of the train were given a double guard.

Captain Stanley was about to call "STRE-ETCH OUT!" when he changed his mind. Running toward the wagon train from the Indian camp were hundreds of Indian women and children. Most of them had never seen a wagon before, and they wanted to come close enough to touch the wagons. Captain Stanley waited a few minutes for them to satisfy their wish to know more about the white man's wagons. The men motioned them back and the teams started forward

slowly. The Indian children's eyes were big with wonder as they saw the wheels turn. Some of them ran after the wagons.

But the Indians did not follow the wagons more than a few hundred feet.

"That's that," said Captain Stanley. "I hope we make it to Santa Fe without meeting any more of them."

But they had not been out of sight of the Indian camp for long when a guard came riding up to Captain Stanley.

"There's a bunch of braves following us," he said.

"As long as they keep their distance, pretend you don't see them," said Captain Stanley. "Don't let anyone fire at them."

They went on their uneasy way. When they reached the place that Captain Stanley thought was the best night camping spot, they formed a good, tight corral. Soon the guards reported that the Indians had turned back.

Darkness came. About an hour later, a guard hurried to Captain Stanley. "Band of Indians coming!" he said.

Every man took his place, ready to defend the camp.

Again Captain Stanley warned against shooting without orders.

About forty shadowy figures on horseback drew near. Suddenly a call came from a guard.

"It's all right, men! They're all women except a few braves who are guarding them. They came to see how we make camp for the night."

This went on through the night and the next day. Small groups of Indians seemed to come into sight each time the wagon train guards looked around. Every now and then a band came to call on the wagoners.

A new worry came to the men. The Cimarron River was dry again. The nearness of the Indians had slowed the wagon train, and there was danger of animals and people being without water again. Captain Stanley, knowing what could happen to the wagon train if they could not find water, decided to risk asking the Indian chief.

The chief was wearing his red coat, as he always did when he called on the wagon train. He seemed pleased to be asked.

"We will lead you," he said in signs.

"Captain Stanley, can we trust him?" one of the lieutenants asked.

"We don't have much choice," he said. "I haven't forgotten what this tribe did to some of our people two years ago, but we can't risk being without water."

The train followed the little band of warriors on horseback. Over ridge after ridge they went, seeming to follow no trail at all. And then, suddenly, there was a flowing river with green grass along its banks.

That night, the animals had the first good pasture they had had in a long time. All the water kegs were filled before darkness came. The Indians, too, were storing water in their jars and buffalo hide "bags." They made camp just a short distance from the wagon camp.

"I wish they'd go away so we could sleep better," one of the men grumbled as he unrolled his blanket inside the crowded corral. "Hardly room for a man to stretch out here with all these animals staked inside the corral."

Another man reminded him, "Your tongue would be black with thirst tonight if it hadn't been for the Indians."

They settled down to fitful sleep. About midnight, everyone in the wagon camp jumped to his feet and reached for his gun. The Indian camp was alive with sound. A sudden wild shriek had brought the men to their feet. Now they felt their scalps prickle as they heard the fearsome sounds that followed. Every Indian's voice seemed to be taking part in the wailing song that rose above the thumping of drums and the stamping of feet.

For an hour that seemed like six the men crouched behind the wagon wheels, waiting, watching. The sounds came no closer. The guards crawled nearer to the Indian camp, peering into the darkness, watching for figures that might creep from the circle of tepees.

As suddenly as it had been broken, the silence of night returned. The guards watched on.

After another half hour had passed, Captain Stanley said, "We may as well get some sleep if we can."

The camp settled down for three or four more hours of uneasy rest. When the eastern sky was streaked with dawn, guards hurried inside the corral.

"Indians coming!" they said.

Instantly, every man was in fighting position again. Captain Stanley stood up on a wagon tongue.

"Go away," he called, and waved his arms to show the braves what he meant. To his surprise, the Indians turned around and went back to their own camp. But sleep was ended, and the men began the morning work. The "Stretch out!" call came before the Indians returned, and the wagons rolled out of camp.

But the wagons had to move through a crowd of Indians. They stepped out of the way of the teams, but men, women and children crowded in as closely as they dared. Slowly, the wagons moved on, but so did the Indians.

All day long it was like that.

"What do they want?" the men asked each other. "What do they plan to do?"

It was a war of nerves. The wagon train could not free itself of the Indians. That night the Indian camp closed around the wagon camp. In their nervousness, the wagoners were short of temper. More than once, fights were stopped only because Captain Stanley brought the men sharply to their senses.

"Do you want them in the camp and upon us?" he asked.

All night he lay awake. "What do they want of us?" he wondered. And then he knew.

In the morning, the braves circled around the wagons. Captain Stanley with his lieutenants went to each man of the company.

"What can you spare from your wagon?" he asked each wagoner.

The wagoners cut lengths of cloth and brought mirrors, iron pots and a few other things they thought the Indians would like. The lieutenants gathered all the things together as Captain Stanley went around the big square. He even went to the Mexican ladies, who gave him a string of pretty beads. He had about fifty dollars' worth of goods piled up when the red-coated chief came to call.

Again the pipe of peace was offered. Again Captain Stanley smoked it. But this time he was wiser. He knew now what he should have done the first time. In peace talks the Indians were always given presents. The chief expected gifts for letting the wagon train go on in peace.

Stanley made a great show of the pile of things he had collected. "These are the gifts with which we salute our brothers," he said.

The chief looked pleased. He took a bright blue bandanna handkerchief from the pile and held it against his red cloth coat. Then he motioned his men to take the gifts. With more puffs on the pipe and a shaking of hands all around, the chief and his braves left.

"Catch up!" Captain Stanley called, and the morning

business of the camp went on as usual. When the wagon train rolled out, no band of Indians followed it.

A few days later, the wagon train .was fired on by a band of about one hundred Indians. But a few charges from the cannon sent the braves away. They did not return.

The train left the desert behind and made its way through the hills around the south end of the mountains.

"*La entrada de la caravana! Los Americanos!*" the natives of Santa Fe shouted when the caravan at last rolled into the city. The trading began.

One of the adventurers who came with the wagon train in his "dearborn" was a young man named Josiah Gregg. He was surprised to see how much the Mexicans paid for American goods, and decided to become a trader himself.

During the long journey, Josiah Gregg wrote page after page about all he saw and all that happened.

It is because of that young man and the book he wrote from his notes that we know the story of "The Indians Who Would Not Go Away" and the adventures of going west with a Santa Fe wagon train.

MARCUS WHITMAN TAKES WHEELS
TO OREGON

The next year, 1832, there was good news about the northern trail that the fur traders followed to the west. A trader named Captain Bonneville had taken wagons all the way to the Green River valley in western Wyoming!

"If wagons can go that far, I see no reason why we can't travel all the way to Oregon with wagons," said Dr. Marcus Whitman. He had already made a horseback journey to Oregon, where some Indians had asked to have white men come to teach them about God and the way the white man lived. Dr. Whitman wanted to go back to teach the Oregon Indians.

In those days, "Oregon" meant all of the northwestern part of what is now United States, north of California and west of the Rockies, and even up into Canada. No one was quite sure who owned it. England and the United States both said they did. No one lived there except some fur traders and the Indians until Dr. Whitman and a missionary named Parker went there to open a mission in 1835.

Dr. Whitman came back east, but not to stay. He married a young lady who wanted to be a missionary, too.

"You don't mean you are going to take Narcissa out to that wilderness to live, Marcus? Surely you wouldn't do that!" his friends said.

"That is exactly what I mean," Dr. Marcus Whitman said, and two days after the wedding they were on the way, with another couple named Spaulding.

A few weeks later, out on the Nebraska plains near the Platte River, a young boy stood staring at the little group of people who were sitting on the ground around some kind of a sheet spread out near their campfire. Sure looked as if they were sitting around a tablecloth. But who ever heard of such a thing on the plains?

He walked a little closer. Yes, they were eating, and two of the people were women. A breeze brought the heavenly smell of a good stew to the boy's nose. Um-m-m-m! To the boy came memories of his mother's kitchen back home. He had had nothing to eat for two days, and he wanted to run to the little camp and ask for some of that good food.

He started forward. Then he saw that a man was walking toward him. The boy stood still, waiting. The man peered out from behind bushy gray whiskers. What did he mean to do? The boy was ready to run, but hunger held him.

The man's voice was sharp as he called, "Who are you? What do you want of us, boy?"

The boy swallowed. The food smelled so good! He said, "Please, sir, can you spare a little powder for my gun? If you can, I can get some meat for myself."

The man was close now, and the boy saw that he was not old, as he had first thought, and that he had blue eyes that seemed to look right inside him.

"What's your name, boy, and where are you going?" the man asked.

"I am Miles Goodyear, and I'm on my way west to become a trapper."

"Humph," was all the man said. He stared at the boy a moment. Then he turned on his heel and walked away. He called back, "Come and sit down. You look as if you could stand some food in you."

Miles did not have to be asked twice. He hurried after the stocky, whiskered man. As he drew near the two neatly dressed ladies, he remembered that he had lost one moccasin and his bare foot was very dirty. So were his buckskin pants, for that matter, and his cloth

coat and shirt were badly torn. He pulled the battered straw hat from his head as all the people stood up, and ran his fingers through his blond hair, which he hadn't combed since he had run away from home.

The man was speaking. "I am Dr. Marcus Whitman, Miles. This is Mrs. Whitman."

Miles found himself looking into the kindest pair of eyes he ever remembered seeing. Mrs. Whitman was pretty, too. Her hair was a golden color. She looked out of place here on the plains!

He met the other people, too. The other lady was Mrs. Spaulding, and the tall man was her husband, the Reverend Spaulding. There was another fellow named Gray, and a fourth man named Dulin. Off to one side were two Indian boys who seemed to be about his own age, sixteen. Miles learned later that the Indian boys had gone east with Dr. Whitman when he came back from Oregon the year before.

Mrs. Whitman was already filling a tin plate for him from the kettle that hung over the fire. Miles saw that the "tablecloth" was a piece of rubber sheeting spread on the ground. Mrs. Whitman pointed to a place beside it.

"Sit down and eat, Miles. It isn't right that a

growing boy should be without a hot supper."

Miles felt tears coming to his eyes. He rubbed at them angrily with one hand as he took the plate.

Dr. Whitman didn't seem so frightening after a while.

"I need someone to help with the animals, boy," he said. Miles saw a little herd of horses, mules and cows a short way from the camp. "We'll give you your keep for the work."

Miles had finished his food and was about to say his thanks, pick up his old rifle, all he owned in the world, and go on his way. Now he knew heaven had sent these people!

"Yes, sir. Thank you, sir," was all he could say.

That night the coyote's howl sounded almost friendly to the boy who had spent many lonely nights on the prairie. In the morning, there was more good food, and then the little group was ready to move on. The Whitmans and Spauldings had two wagons, seventeen head of cattle, fourteen horses and six mules.

Miles and the Indian boys rode herd on the animals as they moved west. He found plenty to do, and when noon came, Mrs. Whitman told him that they were trying to catch up to the fur company wagon train that was ahead of them on the trail. They would travel with the traders as far as the *rendezvous*, the place where the traders took their goods each year to trade for the furs the trappers and the Indians brought to the meeting place.

"Are you going to pack your goods on the horses?"

"Why should we?" Dr. Whitman said. "We have two good wagons, and plenty of strong animals to pull them. We have need for those wagons at our new mission station in Oregon. No, we shall not pack our goods. We shall take the wagons over the mountains to Oregon."

Miles was surprised at the sureness in Dr. Whitman's voice. After all, no one had taken wagons any farther than the Green River valley where the rendezvous was held. And he had heard that the mountain trails farther on got worse and worse.

They found the tracks of the fur traders' wagons after they crossed to the north side of the Platte River. They traveled as fast as they could, even though the sun beat down on them with more heat each day. Some days they traveled all day without seeing a single tree. The cattle were lagging farther and farther behind the horses and mules, and there were many,

many miles to go. Mrs. Spaulding was not very well and rode inside one of the wagons most of the time, but Mrs. Whitman had Miles put her sidesaddle onto a horse each morning and she rode with the men.

At last they caught up with the fur traders. The two wagons became part of a longer train, then. There were seven fur company wagons, each one loaded with trading goods. Teams of six mules pulled each wagon. There were many pack animals, too, and about sixty-five fur company men who rode horseback. There were six men going west for the sport of hunting, too, and each of them had a man to do camp work for him.

Late in the afternoon, whenever a good camping place was reached, the wagons formed a circle for the night. The campfires were built outside the circle, and those who were the cooks set to work. The missionaries put up their tent off to one side.

Mrs. Whitman and Mrs. Spaulding always unrolled their "tablecloth," trying to carry as much of their old life as they could into this wilderness. Miles rather liked it.

Sometimes, after the meal, the missionaries heard singing and laughing from the camps of the fur traders, but usually the camp settled down to sleep as soon as it was dark. At the first touch of gray in the morning sky, the call would come, "Arise! Arise!"

Sometimes the call did not awaken everyone, but it set off a whole herd of four-legged "alarm clocks," for the mules knew that the call meant they would soon be taken out of the wagon corral to feed outside the circle while the people cooked and ate breakfast.

"Ee-aaaw! Ee-aaaw!" they bellowed in forty different tones, and no man could sleep another wink.

Day after day on the trail began this way and went on with mile after mile walked across the treeless plains. Each day, the missionaries' horses seemed to grow weaker and dropped farther behind the mule teams of the fur train.

"We'll have to lighten the loads," Dr. Whitman said. "I shall sell my extra clothes when we get to Fort William."

Narcissa Whitman thought of the pretty dresses she had packed in the little trunk her sister had given her for a present when she was getting ready to leave home. She sighed.

"I shall leave my clothes, too, then."

Fort William came in sight at last. This fort, which was the first building the people had seen since thev left Missouri, would be known as Fort Laramie a little later and be famous as a western outpost for many years. It seemed wonderful to the two women. Even to sit on a chair again made them happy. One of the first things they did was wash their clothes.

Dr. Whitman and Mr. Spaulding were working on one of their wagons when the fur train leader, Thomas Fitzpatrick, came up to them.

"Surely you don't plan to take those wagons any farther," the mountain man said. "We are putting all our goods onto pack animals. From here on we have mountain trails to travel. You can get some good mules here and do the same."

Dr. Whitman straightened up. His mouth was set in a firm line. "Mr. Fitzpatrick, these wagons are going all the way to Oregon."

Thomas Fitzpatrick knew the mountains well. He had trapped beaver in just about every stream in the west. "The wagons will slow you down and make your journey harder. It will be harder for your ladies, too."

"Mrs. Spaulding is ill," Dr. Whitman said. "She must ride in a wagon."

Thomas Fitzpatrick saw the stubborn lines on Dr. Whitman's face. He shrugged his shoulders and turned away. But Dr. Whitman was thinking about what the mountain man had said.

"Spaulding, I think we had better take just one wagon instead of two. We must go through our belongings, leave what we don't really need, and repack the rest into one wagon."

Narcissa gave her pretty dresses to the Indian girls in the fort. The dark skinned girls had never seen a blonde lady before, nor any white woman, for that matter. They followed Narcissa about, wanting to touch her pretty hair. To have her lovely dresses was the most wonderful thing that could have happened to them.

Narcissa packed other things into the little trunk, and on they went.

Dr. Whitman soon saw that Fitzpatrick was right about the road becoming rougher. Often the Whitmans and Spauldings were an hour or two behind the fur traders at day's end.

Mrs. Spaulding often had to get out of the wagon, for it tipped badly on the rocky trail. Sometimes it went over. There were places on the trail where pack animals could go between the trees, but the space was not wide enough for a wagon.

Miles Goodyear often had to cut down a tree so that the wagon could get by.

"Wouldn't it be better to pack your goods onto the horses, Dr. Whitman?" he asked.

Dr. Whitman only said, "I need the wagon. Captain Bonneville took wagons over this trail four years ago. If a fur trader could do it, so can a missionary."

Thomas Fitzpatrick saw the lines deepen on Whitman's face. The women looked more tired each day, too.

"Stubborn fellow," Fitzpatrick said, and he shook his head. No one could talk the man out of taking his wagon through. But Fitzpatrick sent scouts to find the smoothest way for the wagon, even if it meant going around a longer way.

They passed Independence Rock, that huge loaf-shaped rock that stands alone on a plain.

A few days later, they were crossing the Continental Divide.

"This is the backbone of America," Fitzpatrick told Miles. "To the west of this spot, all rivers run toward the Pacific Ocean. To the east, they all find their way to the Gulf of Mexico or into the Atlantic Ocean."

It didn't seem like much of a "backbone" to Miles,

for the land was almost level there. But the travelers had been climbing, day after day, mile after mile, and they were up where the nights are very cold and the sunny summer days are hot.

On the Fourth of July, they went through South Pass. That night, some Indians came into camp from the west. They asked for "men who talked about God." They had a paper for the missionaries.

The letter was from Mr. Parker, another missionary. The plan was that Parker would meet the Whitmans and the Spauldings at the rendezvous to guide them the rest of the way to Oregon.

Dr. Whitman broke the seal and read the letter. "Parker can't come. But he says these Indians will guide us better than he could."

The Indians went back with the missionaries. The chief could speak a little English that he had learned from Parker.

"What this?" he asked, pointing to the wagon. Whitman showed him how easily wheels turned when the horses took a few steps. The Indian was very interested, and he helped get the wagon over the rough parts of the trail from then on.

When they reached the rendezvous, Dr. Whitman

could hardly wait for the women to wash the clothes. He was in a hurry to go on. There were some fur traders there from the Columbia River valley. Dr. Whitman asked if his people could travel with them.

"Sure," they said. Then they saw the wagon.

"You aren't going to take that thing over the mountain trails! Only pack animals can get through," they said.

Dr. Whitman said, "I have been over the trail. I am taking this wagon. We need it at the mission station we plan to build."

One of the two men who had come with the missionaries decided he had had enough. "I'm joining the trappers," he said. "It will be easier than lifting that wagon over the mountains."

But Dr. Whitman's mind was made up. He traded his horses for mules, hitched them to the wagon and they set out again, where no wagon had ever gone before.

They had not gone far when the wagon got stuck in a creek. Then all hands had to help the mules pull it up a steep mountainside. The next day the trail was narrow and slanted and the wagon tipped over twice.

"It can't be done, Dr. Whitman," Miles Goodyear

said. "Please pack the goods on the mules and leave the wagon."

"No," said Dr. Whitman.

A few days later, the axle tree of the front wheels broke.

"Good," thought Narcissa. "Now he will have to leave that foolish wagon and we can get on faster."

But Dr. Whitman still would not give up. He took the wagon apart, so that only the back wheels and axle were left. He fastened the parts that were needed for the mules to pull it like a cart, and then tied the front wheels onto it, so that they made a platform.

"I can't see why you bother with it," Miles said.

"I am going to take these wheels to Oregon," Dr. Whitman said. He found no place to carry his books and some of the other things. They had to be left in the wilderness.

On they went, struggling along mile after mile. Rocks, the biting dust near Soda Springs, the desert, and then a roof again! Fort Hall came into sight.

Miles saw Dr. Whitman tightening up the cart on their day of rest at the fort.

"Dr. Whitman," he said, "you aren't going to take that thing any farther, are you?"

72

"I am," said Dr. Whitman.

Miles thought of the long trail ahead. Then he said, "Dr. Whitman, you've been very kind to me, and I'd like to go to Oregon with you. But if that cart goes on, I'm going to stay here at Fort Hall."

Dr. Whitman had grown fond of Miles, and the boy was a real help on the journey. But his dream of taking wheels to Oregon was too strong to let it die. "Then we'll say good-by here," he said.

Miles watched them head up the trail along Snake River. Then he went into the Fort and asked for a job. Later he became a well known fur trader, and then the first farmer in the state of Utah.

Each day the horses and mules and cattle grew weaker. There was little grass for them to eat. They traveled slowly, and the cart continued to give trouble. The fur traders were worried about how many days their horses could go without better pasture.

"We have to go faster, Dr. Whitman," they said. "Leave your cart and let's get on to good pasture while the animals can still travel."

But all Dr. Whitman would say was, "I'll lighten the load again. Narcissa, my dear, your trunk will have to be left."

Narcissa looked upon the little trunk as her dearest treasure, for it was all she had left of her old life in the east. But she said nothing. As they started out the next morning, she saw the little trunk lying by the trail. One of the fur traders picked it up.

"This is a pretty thing, Dr. Whitman. May I have it?" he asked.

"Of course," said Dr. Whitman. Narcissa watched as the rough mountain man tied it onto the side of his mule.

"Why couldn't my husband have done the same thing?" she thought, but she pushed the thought to one side.

They came to the place where they had to cross the Snake River. The current was fast and it was hard for the horses to walk through the water without slipping. Last of all to cross was Marcus with his cart.

Those who were already on the riverbank watched the mules pick their way over the slippery rocks. They were almost across when one of them slipped. Down they went, and the harness tangled in their legs. Marcus, cart and all seemed about to go downstream with the helpless, struggling animals when the mountain men plunged into the water.

As quickly as they could, they cut the harness to free the animals. Then they helped get the cart and the mules on shore. Dr. Whitman climbed the bank dripping wet.

"Now will you leave that thing?" the fur traders asked.

"I thank you for your help, but having come this far I will not leave it now," Dr. Whitman said.

"I'm sorry, then," one of the men said, "but we shall have to go ahead. We cannot wait while you drag that cart over the trail."

The Indians were still with the missionaries to guide them, so the fur traders went on. Mile after mile, the little group urged their tired animals along the trail. At last there was grass again, and the animals grew stronger. They reached Fort Boise, at the place where the states of Idaho and Oregon touch each other. Three days of rest there, and the missionaries were ready to go on. They headed for a place near the present city of Walla Walla, Washington.

The men at the fort said, "Dr. Whitman, you must leave that cart. You are risking the lives of your people if you try to take it any farther."

Spaulding said, "They are right, Marcus."

"Please, Marcus," said Narcissa.

The Indian chief said, "I take wheels apart. Pack them on horse."

Dr. Whitman sighed. "Yes," he said.

The Indians took the iron tires from around the wheels and flattened them. They bundled spokes into a pack. Dr. Whitman would be able to make new wheels from them with a little work and a hickory sapling when he reached Oregon.

Suddenly, everyone was happier. It was as if they had all been dragging rocks from ropes around their necks. Now they were free. Mrs. Spaulding looked better right away.

There were more deep river crossings, and more narrow escapes. They ran out of food before journey's end. But without the cart to drag, the last miles were miles of hope.

And then, one day, before them lay a valley. Green, green grass waved gently. Beyond the grassy fields, a patch of woods like a park called them to cool shade and rest.

On September 1, 1836, the missionaries reached Fort Walla Walla. Their journey, three and a half months long, was over. And, in a way, Marcus had brought his wheels to Oregon.

JOHN BIDWELL'S GIANT STEP

TO CALIFORNIA

John Bidwell was a restless young man. He read about the new missions in Oregon. He read stories of Kit Carson and other trappers who were exploring the west, clear over to California.

In 1839 the Whitmans had been in Oregon three years. John Bidwell's Ohio home could hold him no longer. He heard of land that the government was selling to settlers in western Missouri, north of Independence and near the Missouri River. This was the first step to adventure. Off he went. He filed a claim and built a log cabin.

One summer day in 1840, John came home to his cabin, just as usual. A moment later he found himself facing the business end of a gun.

"Get out," the man behind the gun said. "This is my claim. I saw it first, and I've come back to take it."

John had no choice. Besides, he had just come from talking with a trapper who had been to far-off California. Even before the gunman jumped his claim,

John wondered if Missouri was where he really wanted to settle down.

"California! That's where I want to go," he told his neighbors. "The Mexican government will give a man a big ranch for little or nothing."

He set to work talking people into taking the giant step to adventure with him. They would travel by wagon.

"Remember, come to Sapling Grove outside of Independence, ready to start for California, by May 9."

The fact that no one had ever gone all the way to California by wagon train did not bother young John. He painted the picture of adventure in such bright colors that five hundred people promised to go.

John was getting his own wagon ready in March, 1841, when a letter was printed in all the newspapers, a letter that spoiled his plans. It was from a man who had gone to California the year before, and now was back east. His words about California made a black picture.

"I'm not going, if that is what California will be like," said one of the men who planned to take his family in John's wagon train.

"Count me out, too," said another.

"The same for me," "and me," "and me."

John lost all his company. All that was left was his own wagon. The team to pull it was to have been furnished by another young man.

Just when it seemed that even John would have to give up, a man rode into Independence on a fine black horse.

"Where is the California company?" he asked. "I'm ready to go."

Someone sent him over the Missouri River to Liberty, the frontier town where John lived.

John said, "Trade your horse for some oxen and I'll share my wagon with you."

"I've come this far, so I may as well," George Henshaw said. He traded his horse for a pair of oxen and got a one-eyed mule in the bargain.

"The mule won't be as fine to ride as my horse was, but it will do," said Henshaw. "When do we start, Bidwell?"

"The ninth day of May is the day we set. Maybe other wagons will be waiting for us in Independence," John said.

The two men loaded the wagon with supplies and took the ferry over the river, wagon, oxen, mule and all. Sure enough, a family with a wagon was waiting at Sapling Grove.

California fever was not entirely gone. Seeing two wagons loaded and ready to go helped bring it back to a few people. John and his new partner talked to everyone they met, and when the day came to leave, sixty-nine men, women and children were willing to go. With them were thirteen wagons and an assortment of animals.

These people were taking a giant step. They had very little money, no leader who had been west before, and maps that were drawn from guesses about most of the land between the Green River and California. The maps showed two large rivers flowing west, right through the mountains, from an oversize Great Salt Lake to the Pacific Ocean. One of the rivers was called the River Buenaventure. It was on all the old maps, beginning with those the Spaniards had made, but no one had ever seen it.

"We'll follow one of those river valleys, and we can find our way easily," said hopeful John. "But let's elect a captain to be in charge of the wagon train."

A big fellow named John Bartleson stepped forward.

He had come into the camp at the last minute, bringing seven strong men with him.

"I'll be the captain," he said. "I'll be the captain, or my men won't go."

Bidwell knew that every man would be needed. "You're the captain, Bartleson," he said. So the wagon train was known as the Bartleson-Bidwell train.

Luck took a hand soon. The thirteen wagons caught up with some priests and their workmen who were going to Oregon to be missionaries. Not only had their leader, Father DeSmet, been to Oregon the year before, but he had hired Thomas Fitzpatrick, the trapper, to go with them as a guide.

"Why don't we travel together until our trails part?" Father DeSmet asked.

John liked the priest. "He looks like a shiny red apple on a black pillow," was his first thought. Then he saw that the round red face had the lines that tell of a great life, and the black robe covered the body of a man who was short and fat but as strong as a blacksmith.

The priests carried their goods in four two-wheeled carts with hoops over them like covered wagons. Each cart was pulled by a pair of mules hitched one behind the other. Another wagon joined the train soon after. By the time they reached the Platte River valley, about eighty people were traveling together.

They reached buffalo country and enjoyed fresh meat again. But one day, they found themselves in the path of a great herd of buffalo, thundering toward them. The herd was about a mile away. Thomas Fitzpatrick was the only one who knew what to do to keep the whole wagon train from being run over.

"Run for it!" Bartleson cried, but Fitzpatrick galloped back to the men, waving his arms.

"No! You can't outrun the buffalo. Gather buffalo chips, dry grass and anything that will burn and build a row of fires."

Fires were built quickly between the oncoming buffalo and the wagons.

Trembling from fear and the hurried work, the people huddled behind their wagons and watched the buffalo draw near. The earth rumbled with the beat of a thousand hoofs on the hard-baked prairie. Many covered their heads, expecting to feel those pounding hoofs upon them any moment.

And then they were an island in a moving brown sea. The herd parted in the middle to stay clear of the fires. The pounding sea was all around them, and then it was gone.

One day, they were sure they were about to be attacked by Indians. Again Fitzpatrick took command. He had taught the travelers to move in a double line that could quickly form a circle. In a few minutes he had the wagon train ready to meet the Indian band riding toward them.

Then the old trapper galloped out of the circle and headed toward the Indians. He held up his hand in the sign of peace. He smoked the pipe of peace with the chief and a few minutes later the war party rode off.

John Bidwell fingered the rifle he had been ready to use and almost wished there had been a battle. It would have been exciting! Then he realized that a battle would have meant death to some of his party. He was grateful for Fitzpatrick's help.

Some days they only plodded on. Other days there were adventures for John to remember. There was the day a wagon tipped over when they were crossing the North Fork of the Platte River. The wagon drifted down the river while mules and men splashed about wildly. But wagon, men and all but one mule made it to shore.

There were thunderstorms on the plains that outdid any storm John had ever seen. Quicksand in some of the rivers made crossings dangerous. Even Fitzpatrick became lost for a few days in a desert stretch and it seemed as if people and animals would die before they found water again. But just in time, the old trapper found the valley of the Green River, and the train was saved.

This was the first year that the fur companies were not holding the big rendezvous. It was there in the strangely empty Green River valley that some of the Bartleson-Bidwell people decided that they would go to Oregon with Father DeSmet instead of to California. They reached the place where Bear River swings south toward Great Salt Lake. There the Oregon party, including Fitzpatrick, went on toward Fort Hall, while the California travelers followed Bear River to the south.

Fitzpatrick looked over Bidwell's maps and marked changes on them.

"There is no River Buenaventura," he said. "Jed Smith almost lost his life looking for it fifteen years ago. There are mountains the Spanish call the Sierra Nevadas at the south, running all along the eastern edge of California. North of them, running through the Oregon country, are the Cascade Mountains." Then the mountain man showed John where to find the best place to get over the mountains.

Fitzpatrick gave the California travelers good advice that made it possible for them to travel alone. They shook hands all around, and the thirty-two who wanted to go to California were on their own. Among them were young Mr. and Mrs. Ben Kelsey who had a tiny baby girl.

John felt that old excitement stirring in him at the thought of new dangers and adventures. The way ahead would not be easy, but he looked forward to it.

That night there seemed to be so few of them as they gathered around the campfire. They missed cheerful Father DeSmet and wise old Tom Fitzpatrick.

"We'll make it," John said. He touched Ben Kelsey's shoulder as they went to the wagons for their bed rolls. "Don't worry, Ben. You'll be glad you came when you see your daughter growing up as the belle of California."

A day or two later, John's urge for adventure almost got him lost in the mountains. It was a hot summer day. The wagon train seemed to crawl along through the Bear River valley. It was George Henshaw's turn to handle the ox team, and John was walking near the end of the train with an eighteen-year-old boy named Jimmy John.

"Sure is hot," Jimmy said. He wiped the sweat from his brow. Then he pointed to a snow-capped mountain which rose to the west. "Just think how good that snow would feel right now."

John grinned. "Why don't we go and get some, Jimmy?"

Jimmy said, "I'm game. Come on. We'll go and get some and bring it back to the wagon train before they miss us."

Their eyes met, and instantly they both knew they were not joking. "It looks to be an hour's walk from here," Jimmy added.

"Let's go," said John, and the two left the trail. They forgot the heat in the excitement of adventure, and almost ran towards the mountain. A steep climb up a foothill slowed them down before long. And when they reached the top of the hill, they saw there was a broad valley between them and the mountain.

"It's farther than I thought, Jimmy" said John. "Maybe we'd better go back to the wagon train. Neither of us has a gun with us."

Jimmy said nothing, but the look he gave John spoke for him. "You're afraid," it said. The boy turned his back on John and headed down the slope into the valley.

"Jimmy! Come back!" John yelled. But Jimmy ran faster. John, left alone, did not know what to do.

"Well, all right. If you think I'm afraid, I'll show you," he said aloud, and ran after Jimmy.

Before the two reached the bottom of the valley, the sun had dropped behind the mountains and the shadows were long. But the boys went on, side by side.

"Remember how hot we were a little while ago?" Jimmy asked. "I wish I had a coat now. The nights sure get cold in these mountains."

John made up his mind not to say another word about going back. If Jimmy suggested it, he would go back. But Jimmy walked on. They were both hungry and tired, but on they went. As night came on, they saw something that added fear to their feelings. Not far up the valley they saw Indian campfires.

They stumbled on in the darkness, fighting their way up a sharp ridge which marked the beginning of the climb to the snow on the mountain. Too tired to talk, they fought their way over rocks and through brush. The sharp rocks cut through their moccasins, and the pain was almost more than either young man could stand. They crawled more than they walked then, but on and upward they went until at last they were too tired to go on.

"The moon has set," John said. "It must be past midnight." The darkness was broken only by darker shapes that were fir trees growing high on the mountain side.

They crawled to the shelter of a tree and pulled their shirts tight about them to hold in the warmth of their bodies. Side by side, they lay down under the tree.

What's all this fuzzy stuff on the ground?" Jimmy asked.

John felt soft hairs, about two or three inches long.

"We're in a spot that's been slept in before," he said. "Grizzly bears!"

Jimmy shivered.

"Hope they have another nest for tonight," he said.

They lay there, waiting for the first light of the new day. Neither of them slept. At the first streak in the east, they crawled out from under the tree and stood on their stone-bruised, cut feet.

"There's just one good thing about being half frozen," Jimmy said. "I can hardly feel the cuts on my feet.'

John thought they would surely head down the mountain now, but Jimmy turned in the direction of the snow. An hour or two later they reached it.

"How hard it is," Jimmy said as he tried to scoop up some snow.

"The sun probably melts the top of it a little each day, and then it freezes again at night," John said. "Let's fill up our handkerchiefs with it and get on our way down toward the wagon train. I think we can find an easier way than over all those rocks we climbed in the dark."

They were too tired to look around at the beautiful scene spread before them. Each had a large bandanna handkerchief, and as soon as it was well packed with snow, they began the downward trip.

There wasn't any easy way down the mountain. They missed the rocky ridge, but in its place there were tangles of brush and woods so thick that the sunshine couldn't get in. There were places where grizzly bears had shouldered their way through. The boys crawled along these brambly tunnels.

In one place, they found they were close on the heels of a bear, for they saw his wet tracks on the steep bank of a wild little mountain stream they had to plunge through.

"Keep your knife ready, Jimmy," John said. "Mr. Bear could smell us coming and turn around to meet us."

"And don't forget those Indians waiting in the valley," Jimmy said.

Knives drawn, they went on their painful way.

Down at the wagon train, the men had drawn together in council. John and Jimmy had been missed, of course, as soon as Bartleson had called for a stop for the night. When morning came and there was no sign of them, some of the men had gone back to look for them. Now it was almost noon, and all were back from searching.

Faces were glum around the circle.

"Likely the Indians came up on them at the end of the train," one man said.

"Well, let's get on our way, then," said Bartleson. "No use waiting here for them to kill all of us."

Ben Kelsey said, "But if they are alive and they find

their way back to the trail, think how awful it would be for them if they didn't find us."

"We're going," said Bartleson. "Catch up!" he called.

In silence, the men hitched their teams to the wagons, and in a little while the train was moving south once again. They had gone two or three miles when the man who brought up the rear heard a faint call. He looked out over the valley and saw two figures waving wildly.

"Stop the train, Bartleson! Here they come," he yelled.

Teams stopped, and half the people ran toward John and Jimmy.

"Where have you been?" they cried when they were near enough.

The clothes of the two adventurers hung in tatters. They were scratched and cut and their faces were lined with tiredness, but both grinned as they held out wet bandannas.

John said, "We have been up to the snow. See?" and he opened the wet handkerchief. In it was the proof, a tiny snowball.

Even John had lost his longing for adventure long

before they reached California. Each day, as they went on, there was enough adventure just in staying alive and moving on. Often the travelers wished they had Tom Fitzpatrick there to help them choose the way to go.

They struggled over mountains and deserts. At the western edge of Utah, they had to leave their wagons and "pack" the rest of the way. But they made it over the last mountains to the Sacramento Valley before winter snows blocked their way.

Ben Kelsey's wife and baby suffered on the trip, but they lived through it. Just as Narcissa Whitman and Mrs. Spaulding were the first women to travel overland to Oregon, Mrs. Kelsey was the first woman to make the long journey to California from the Missouri River.

As for John Bidwell, his "giant step" to adventure was all he needed to make him a solid citizen of California. He settled down on a ranch, and many years later John Bidwell ran for President of the United States.

The Bartleson-Bidwell wagons did not travel all the way to the Pacific, but just as others followed the Whitmans to Oregon and took wagons all the way, so wagon trains soon reached California.

ALEC MAJOR'S WANDERING OXEN

Alec Majors had been in the Santa Fe freighting business for two years, but never had he found himself in such danger as on that morning in early June, 1850.

By that time, the United States reached all the way to California. Oregon, too, had become part of the United States when the arguments with England over the borders were settled. The Oregon Trail, the California Trail and the Santa Fe Trail were roadways now, and no longer did wagons have to be taken apart to get them over the mountains to the Pacific.

When Alec Majors went to St. Louis to buy some of the big Conestogas so that he could take freight to Santa Fe, one of the men standing about the wagon company's yards looked at him as if he were crazy.

"Don't you think it's foolish to put all your money into a dying business?" he asked Mr. Majors.

"Dying? Why, carrying freight across the plains is just beginning to be important. Just to take supplies to the soldiers who are in the western forts will take many, many loads of goods. The hundreds of people who have gone to live in Oregon and California need goods, too, and they can't always wait for it to come all the way around South America by boat."

Alec Majors went on choosing his wagons. When he left St. Louis, he had six big Conestogas. He bought oxen to pull them because he believed they could pull heavier loads for more hours a day than mules or horses could, even though they traveled more slowly. Oxen could pull a wagon out of a muddy river bottom when mules and horses gave up. He found men who were willing to help him drive his wagon train. He was in business.

That was the year 1848. Later that year news came from California that filled the United States with excitement.

"Gold! They've found gold in California!"

When spring came in 1849, the stream of wagons heading west turned into a flood. By the end of June, almost 6,000 wagons had gone by Fort Kearney on the Platte River. And the next year there were even more.

Alec Major's freighting business was better than ever. He had more wagons and more men working for him every month. But on that June morning in 1850, his wagon trains nearly lost their leader.

Alec himself was wagon-master for the freight train. His ten Conestogas creaked and groaned their slow way over the hard packed Santa Fe Trail for about ten days. Six pairs of oxen pulled each wagon. There were extra oxen being driven along behind the wagons, too, for often an animal became lame and could not work.

At night, the train made camp as usual. The oxen were unharnessed in the corral formed by the wagons and then taken out to feed for the night on the good grass. They were in what is now western Kansas but was then called Indian Territory.

Alec Majors usually put men on guard duty to watch the oxen through the night, but this night he did not.

"We've had a long, hard day," he told his men. "The best grass is right here near our camp, and the animals are too tired to wander very far away. We're all tired, for that matter. Let's all get a good night's rest."

The wagon-master was the first man up the following morning. He was saddling his horse, getting ready to ride out to drive the oxen into the corral when his assistant came over to him.

"Morning, Mr. Majors," said the assistant. "Want me to round up the cattle for you?"

"Thanks, Sam," said Alec, "but I'm nearly ready. You get the men up. I'll have the oxen in the corral as soon as the men are ready for them."

Alec liked the sounds of early morning and the feel of the fresh, cool air. As he rode out of the corral, a meadow lark sang its cheerful good morning. Far off across the rolling green of the plains, a line of slender antelopes drank from one of the streams that ran through the gulches.

The man breathed deeply, enjoying it all. Then the red rim of the sun peeped over the curving land to the east to remind him that time was passing and he'd best be getting the oxen rounded up. Soon the morning freshness would be gone and the day would settle into a slow, plodding push through the heat of summer on the treeless plains.

He circled behind the last animals.

"Get along there!" he called out, and the animals turned toward the others. Soon there was a dark, solid group of oxen. When they turned toward the corral Alex realized there were not as many oxen as there should be.

"Some of them must be over the next rise of land," he thought.

He left the herd and circled around, looking for tracks. He soon found a trail of hoof marks and galloped off.

But the oxen were not over the next rise. Alec had gone a mile or so when he noticed that hoof prints of ponies were among those of the oxen.

"Indian ponies!" he said aloud. "So! They drove off my oxen so I'd pay them to find them for me and bring them back. I'll catch up and send them on their way!"

He knew of no unfriendly Indians in that part of the territory, so it did not worry him that he did not have a gun with him. He galloped on, following the trail.

When he had traveled several miles, he began to wish some of his men were with him. The sun was well up in the sky, and still the trail went on.

About twelve miles from the wagon camp, Alec came to a little stretch of woods. He rode through it, and just beyond he saw his oxen resting.

"They must be worn out," Alex thought. "They traveled all day, and they must have walked most of the night, too. I'll not get them to travel far today. Believe me, from now on I'm posting a guard."

Then he saw them—six painted Indian braves, each standing beside his horse, ready to mount. A sudden sinking feeling went through Alec's body. These men were not from the friendly tribes he knew. He saw the guns held ready in the Indians' hands, and thought of his foolishness in coming so far unarmed.

He felt six pairs of black eyes watching him as he galloped to his oxen and circled about them.

"Yah-OOOO! Get back there! Yah-OOOooo!" he yelled, sounding as fierce as he could. The oxen, surprised, began to head back on the trail toward the little stretch of woods. There were thirty-four of them.

Alec kept shouting as he galloped after the bellowing oxen. He pretended he did not see the six Indians. His back was to them now, and it fairly prickled with the bullet he was sure would come flying after him. The oxen entered the woods. Alec, on his horse, followed.

No bullet whizzed after him. The cattle came to the edge of the woods and out into the open plain. There was no sound of horsemen behind Alec as he drove the oxen.

"Well, I must say that went well," he thought in surprise.

Then, about a half-mile ahead, he saw the figure of a man on horseback coming toward him. He thought it was one of his own men, coming to help him.

"And about time," he said. Then he saw that the figure was that of an Indian. Alec stiffened. But when the lone rider was a short distance from the herd, he left the trail and circled around the animals and Alec. Alec saw him return to the trail and go on toward the woods.

The same thing happened again and again. But no one tried to stop Alec and his slow moving herd. On they went.

"It pays to make a brave front before those fellows," Alec decided. "Looks as if they are going to let me go."

A few minutes later he was not so sure. He looked ahead, and coming over the next rise of ground were not just one or two riders, but a large band of Indian braves. Alec guessed there were about twenty-five in the party, and he saw that they were armed and painted for war. On they came. They did not swing off the trail.

As they drew near, Alec felt much smaller than he had a few minutes before and he found his bravery shrinking, too. Even with a gun, he would have stood little chance against a party like this. The chief carried a gun. The other braves held arrows ready to fire from their bows.

Suddenly, the braves let out a horrible yell. Their

ponies rushed toward the oxen at top speed. If the oxen had not been so tired, they would have stampeded. They tried to run, but slowed down as Alec galloped his horse around them. Oxen and Indian ponies came face to face and stopped. Alec found himself looking into the barrel of the chief's rifle.

Quickly, he wheeled his horse and galloped out of the gun's reach to give himself time to think.

"He's trying to scare me away from my herd so that he can have them all," Alec decided. "I can't go on without the oxen."

He rode back toward his herd, but the chief spurred his pony and came charging. Alec backed off again. Three times Alec tried to get to his herd, and three times the chief rode toward him, gun held ready to fire. Most of the other braves got off their ponies and were dancing and yelling around the frightened, bellowing oxen. The wild sounds and his own helplessness, Alec felt his nerves tighten. If only his men would come riding over the ridge! What could they be doing all this time?

Now the chief sat quietly on his horse near the herd, between it and Alec. He seemed to be waiting for Alec's next move. Slowly, cautiously, Alec rode toward him. The chief made signs for him to come near.

Wondering what was to happen next, Alec rode up slowly until his horse was beside the chief's, facing the same way. As soon as he stopped, the brave who was sitting on a pony on the other side of the chief, slid to the ground. Quickly he ducked under the head of the chief's horse and reached for Alec's bridle.

"Oh, no!" Alec cried and pulled his horse back. Again he galloped off, circled and came back, watching for the chief's next move.

Again the signal came from the chief for Alec to ride near to him. Alec's heart told him to ride away while he could and forget his oxen, but if he did, he would be out of business, for the Indians would try again and again. He rode toward the chief.

This time, the brave took a position on the chief's left side so that he was between Alec and the chief. Again all three horses faced the same way. Alec glanced at the brave's face. The terrible look of hatred in the eyes of the brave sent a chill through Alec. He looked down at the brave's brown hands. The veins in them stood out as the Indian held the steel-tipped arrow in a full-drawn bow. It was aimed directly at Alec's heart.

A cold sweat broke out on Alec's brow. He could feel

a cramping around his heart where that arrow would hit. Was this to be the end? He could not talk with the Indians except in sign language. He did not know their tongue and they seemed to know no English.

Except for one word. As he held the bow ready to send the arrow on its short, sure journey, the brave spat out the word, "Say!"

Alec's eyes looked into the brave's questioningly. But all he saw was burning coals of hate. He looked at the chief. The chief put his gun under one arm and held up ten fingers. Alec felt the tightness leave his body. Though he knew the brave would gladly kill him, the chief was willing to bargain, and the chief's wish was law.

Later, Alec wondered why he didn't give the Indians ten oxen and get away quickly. But he knew he could not get his train to Santa Fe if he gave up ten oxen, and he shook his head and said, "No."

Five fingers of one hand closed around the chief's gun. He held up the five fingers of the other hand toward Alec. The brave made a move as if to let the arrow fly. Still Alec held out. He shook his head. He would not give away five oxen.

The chief's questioning look and wave of his hands

showed Alec that he was to make an offer. He held up one finger.

Alec never understood why the chief settled so cheaply. Probably he was nervous about some party of soldiers he knew were near by, or perhaps he felt Alec would only be so brave if he knew his men were ready to attack. But he nodded his head, spoke a command to his braves and the dance around the herd ended.

It was over in a moment. The Indians took one fine ox and rode toward the woods. Alec was free! He looked around, sure that his men must be just over the ridge and that the Indians had seen them coming.

But they were not. Alec reached camp in the early afternoon with his thirty-three oxen. He was almost afraid of what he would find there. Surely the men had been attacked or they would have come looking for him. But there they were, leaning against the wagons, just as if he'd been gone only an hour or so. They came forward only when they saw Alec and the oxen.

"What happened, boss?" Sam called out. "You said you'd be right back!"

Alec sputtered. He couldn't find words to say how he felt, for he was not a man to swear or even yell at his men. But when words came, he fairly roared. "Why didn't you come to help me? I could have been killed!"

A harder working band of wagoners was never seen than those that went on with that journey. When buffalo stampeded the oxen one night a little later, Alec didn't have to lift a finger to get the animals back. All went well the rest of the way to Santa Fe.

The goods brought $13,000 in Mexican silver dollars. Alex paid his men and put aside what his own family needed. With the rest he bought more wagons and more oxen, and more goods to take to the west. To a strong, brave man, good fortune seemed to come by the law of the right, and Alec Majors became "king" of the western freighters.

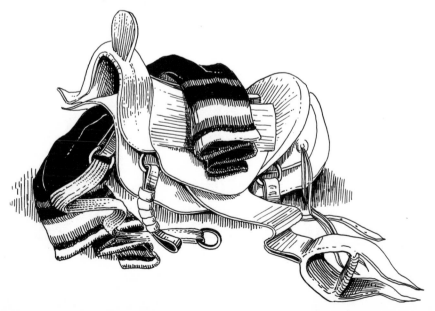

BILLY CODY, WAGON BOY

Ever since his father had brought the Cody family to live near the big army post of Fort Leavenworth, Kansas, near the Missouri River, little Billy Cody had loved to watch the wagon trains heading west. Alec Majors' freighters began their trips at Fort Leavenworth in the days after 1854 since most of their business was hauling goods for the army. Billy used to ride his pony to the wagon trail that ran not far from his log house frontier home. As he watched the "ships of the prairie" heading west, he dreamed of the day when he would be old enough to go along.

"I'm old enough now," he decided when he was eleven. His father died only a few weeks before, and Billy was the "man" of the Cody family. His mother and sisters needed money.

On a day in early summer, 1857, Billy and his mother went into the town of Leavenworth. It had taken Billy hours of talking to get his mother to say he could ask "Uncle Alec" for a job. But now they headed for the building with the big sign that read, *Russell, Majors*

111

& *Waddell.* Alec Majors had partners in his freighting business, now, and there were so many men working for the company that Alec no longer went with the wagon trains himself.

Alec was in his office. He smiled at the handsome brown-eyed boy who stood before him.

"What can you do on a wagon train, Billy?" he asked.

Billy's voice was eager. "I can ride as well as a man, Uncle Alec. I can shoot, too, and drive a team."

"That's work for strong men, Billy," said Alec Majors. "You are only eleven years old, and small for your age at that. Crossing the plains is dangerous work."

He saw the look of disappointment on the boy's face. Then he remembered watching the lad riding his pony as if boy and animal were one.

"But there is an opening you might fill," he added. Up came Billy's head, his eyes bright with new hope. Alec went on.

"I need a messenger boy to carry orders from one section of the trains to another. I'll let you try it. If you can do a man's work, you'll get a man's pay."

The very next day, Billy Cody was on his pony,

Prince, waiting for the moment when the wagon wheels would roll. Strapped to his saddle was his blanket roll with his extra shirt and the few things he would need, and in his holster hung the old muzzle-loading rifle that had been his father's.

At last the long whips cracked out over the heads of the ox teams. The big animals leaned into their yokes and the iron-rimmed wheels began to turn. The wagon train was on its way! It was all Billy could do to keep from galloping his pony full speed ahead and shouting for joy.

But the animals moved slowly, and at the end of the first day's journey they were only twelve miles out of Leavenworth. Billy watched the men make camp. At a call from wagon-master, Frank McCarthy, the twenty-five wagons moved into a big circle. The ox teams seemed to know just how near to the next wagon they should be as they swung the wagon tongues to the inside of the circle. Each wagoner hooked his log chain from the back wheel of his wagon to the front wheel of the next wagon. Then, with the animals safely inside the corral, he set about caring for them.

It was a busy time. The whole camp was divided into "messes" of six to ten men. Each mess had its own cook and the cook set about his work as soon as the circle formed. Another man brought fuel for the fire and water for cooking and for the men to drink. Others rode out of the corral with the cattle. They would ride guard while the animals ate meadow grass and drank from a near-by stream. Each man usually took two hours of guard duty each night.

Billy took care of his horse, staking him out after unsaddling him, as he saw the other extras doing.

It was exciting to sit on the ground near the campfire and eat his supper from a tin plate and drink hot, bitter coffee from a tin cup, just as the wagoners did.

Darkness came and the world closed in on the circle of white-topped wagons, while ever-changing light from the campfires flickered on their sides. Sparks flew up into the blackness, and beyond was a world of mystery. Billy shivered a little and the men teased him about being away from his mother.

After a while the men unrolled their blankets near the wagon. Billy chose a spot not far from a dying campfire. Coyotes sang to the moon and the oxen lowed. The boy heard the snoring of the men around him and found comfort in their nearness. He fell asleep at last, and awoke to the braying of the mules and the shouts of men's voices. The sky was gray with the first light of the second day on the trail.

The cook was putting the smoke-blackened coffee pot over the fire. Billy rolled up his blanket, afraid to speak of the aches in his muscles from the long hours of riding and the hardness of the ground that had been his bed.

In the days that followed, Billy Cody proved to the wagoners that he had the makings of a good man. The train followed the same trail that the fur traders and the Whitmans followed so many years before, swinging northwest from Kansas into Nebraska, and following the Platte River valley. They passed Fort Kearney, and Billy began to feel like an old timer on the wagon train.

He saw and felt one of the thunder storms he had heard so much about. He knew the feel of the wind that never seemed to rest, and the burning heat of the sun on the open prairie. He saw his first herds of buffalo, and helped round up stampeding cattle. He crossed rivers that ran deep and fast with high waters of early summer. There had been no trouble with Indians and it seemed that the train would go on peacefully to Fort Laramie.

But twenty miles west of Fort Kearney, trouble found

them. The noon stop that day was near a creek that ran between steep mud banks, headed toward the Platte. The men unhitched the teams, watered them and staked them out on the grass beyond the circle of wagons.

While the cooks worked, most of the men stretched out to rest in the shade under the wagons. Bill Cody was too hungry to lie down. Instead, he watched the cook of his mess as he worked, cooking bacon, beans and coffee.

Suddenly the peaceful quiet was broken. From a little grove of trees just beyond the three men who rode guard on the cattle, there came a whine of bullets and the bang of rifle fire. Then came a wild yell that made the hair on the back of Billy's neck prickle. The three guards fell from their horses.

"On your feet, men!" Frank McCarthy yelled. Men were already rolling out from under the wagons and reaching for their rifles. A band of yelling Indians, riding hard on their ponies, came into view. The men crouched between the wagons, rifles cocked and ready.

"Fire!" cried McCarthy, and rifles brought down an Indian or two. Other Indians swung away, out of reach of bullets, but not before they had sent a shower of steel-tipped arrows into the camp. Several wagon train men were wounded. The men saw the Indian band swing back around the low hill that had hidden them. The frightened oxen had broken away from their stakes and were scattering over the plain.

"Be ready for them, men! They'll be back in a minute!" called McCarthy. And in a moment, an even larger band of Indians came charging. Billy took his place with the men, loading and firing his old rifle.

"You don't scare worth a penny, do you, Billy?" Frank McCarthy said when the charge was over. He gave the boy a pat on the shoulder and a grin before he turned to meet the next charge.

When the Indians turned away, more men were wounded.

"We can't hold out," said McCarthy. "Our only chance is to get back to Fort Kearney. Take your ammunition and head for the creek. The banks will make a better fort than the wagons. When the next charge is over, we'll wade our way to the Platte."

Helping the wounded along, the wagoners slid down the high creek banks. But there was no way to save the wagons.

"Here they come!" yelled McCarthy.

Guns pointed over the creek banks and the men met

the charge. Most of the Indian arrows fell harmlessly into the deserted wagon camp.

"Now, make time down the creek," McCarthy ordered. "They'll be back soon."

It was slow going, for the men did not want to leave the wounded men behind. Faintly at first came dreaded yelling that meant another charge. When it filled the air, the men pressed against the banks peering over the edge only long enough to fire. As the Indians swung back again, the men lost no time in getting farther down the creek. They reached the Platte and turned eastward. But McCarthy saw that the wounded could not go much farther.

"We'll stop long enough to build a raft for the wounded men," he ordered. Guards were posted and the rest of the men worked as fast as they could cutting small trees that grew along the river and lashing them together with bits of rope and tough vines that grew near the banks. The raft was ready. The wounded men were helped onto it.

"Room for you, too, Billy," the men said.

Billy shook his head. "I'm not wounded. I can walk as well as anyone, and I can swim through the deep places."

They set out again, guiding the raft along as they waded. The current helped move the raft a little, but the river bottom was soft and muddy and the men could not move very fast. Sometimes they found room to walk at the river's edge without showing themselves over the banks. Other times the water was deep and they had to swim. By late afternoon they were all very tired. The Indians seemed to have given up the attack.

"They are having a good time going through our freight," McCarthy said. "We'll go back tomorrow to see what's left. But now we'll head for the fort."

The sun dropped low behind them.

"Sure wish I had some of those beans we left at the camp," Billy thought, but he said nothing. Everyone else must be hungry, too.

Darkness came, and Billy's legs were too tired for him to keep up with the men any longer. But he would not ask to ride on the raft. No one noticed when he stopped a few minutes to rest. The others moved on ahead.

The moon, almost full, rose ahead of them, like a huge gold coin coming up from the river. Billy watched it as he rested. In a few minutes, the gold changed to silver and the river had a lovely shimmering roadway.

"I must move on," the boy thought. "I'd hate to be

caught here alone if the Indians come back." His eyelids were heavy and he shook his head to wake himself. Then he began to move on after the men, almost lost to him now in the shadow of the river's edge.

He tried to reach that silver, winking roadway in the river, but it never seemed any nearer. Then, feeling himself falling asleep, Billy jerked his head up. Instantly, he came to life. Sharply outlined against the moon was a feathered headdress.

"Bang!" his rifle rang out. There was a splashing sound and a call of "Where's little Billy Cody?" Men came toward him. The feathered head was gone and the moon shone down as before.

Some say that Billy only thought he saw an Indian there. Others say the boy really did kill an Indian that night, a scout sent to see where the wagoners had gone.

The man who first reached Billy heard the boy say, "I saw an Indian and I shot him!"

He hurried the boy toward the other men and called out, "Little Billy's killed an Indian all by himself!"

Just before dawn, the tired, hungry men straggled into Fort Kearney. Those who were able, went back to the creek bank the next day on borrowed army mules. All they found was ashes and a few useless wagon parts.

There was nothing to do but to make their way back to Leavenworth.

The story of Billy Cody and the Indian was told over and over and it grew better with the telling. The Leavenworth newspaper printed the story of "the youngest Indian fighter on the plains."

Billy could hardly wait to head west again. Mr. Majors sent him to see the wagon-master of a train that was forming.

"Can you use me?" Billy asked.

The man grinned. "We always can use a good Indian fighter," he said, and Billy was hired.

For the next two or three years, Billy Cody worked on the wagon trains during the summer months. Then Russell, Majors and Waddell had something more exciting for him to do. They needed riders for the new Pony Express. Billy was fourteen years old then, and was probably the youngest rider of them all. This was the open door to more adventures, and from then on, Billy Cody and the Wild West spent their lives together. Billy Cody became known as *Buffalo Bill.*

The days of the wagon trains were numbered. Though more freight than ever was to move west in the years after the War Between the States, a faster, surer way of carrying it was coming. The Iron Horse came snorting, mile after mile across the plains, farther and farther each year. Where the wagon trains had struggled to get over the mountains, tunnels were cut and tracks were laid. In 1869, railroad tracks reached all the way across the United States.

The big, white-topped Conestogas went on for a while with the work they had begun so long ago on the Pennsylvania roads. But each year there were fewer. Their work was done.

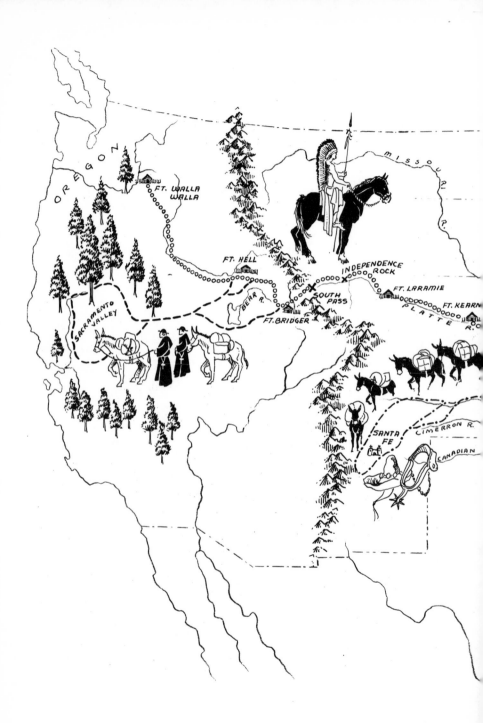

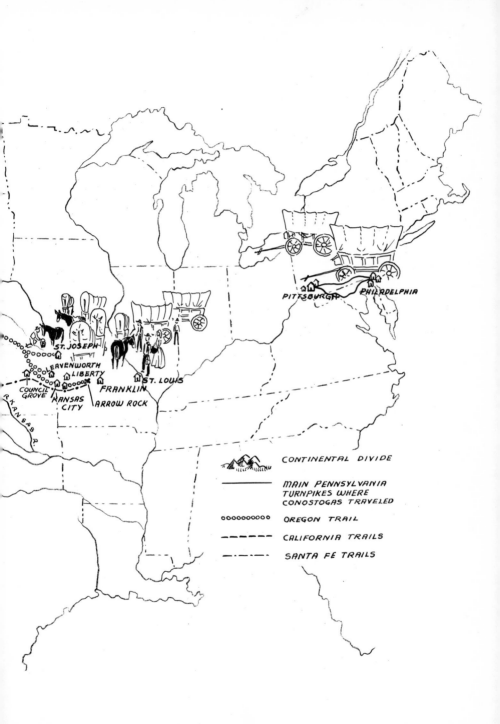

PITTSBURGH   PHILADELPHIA

ST. JOSEPH

LEAVENWORTH
LIBERTY
COUNCIL
GROVE
KANSAS
CITY   FRANKLIN   ST. LOUIS
              ARROW ROCK

R KANSAS R

CONTINENTAL DIVIDE

MAIN PENNSYLVANIA
TURNPIKES WHERE
CONOSTOGAS TRAVELED

ooooooooo OREGON TRAIL

— — — CALIFORNIA TRAILS

—·—·— SANTA FE TRAILS

Edith McCall, in her FRONTIERS OF AMERICA *books, writes in simple uncluttered text without losing the dramatic impact of her true stories of real people. Her purpose is to make these stories of our country available to younger readers and still vital and interesting to a wide age range.*
Mrs. McCall now lives in the Ozarks and writes for children. For many years, she was a reading consultant in LaGrange, Illinois.